はじめての えじてん
どうぶつ

First Picture Dictionary
Animals

ぶた
Pig

うさぎ
Rabbit

ちょうちょ
Butterfly

きつね
Fox

え：あな・いばにーる

www.kidkiddos.com
Copyright ©2025 by KidKiddos Books Ltd.
support@kidkiddos.com

All rights reserved. No part of this book may be reproduced in any form or by any electronic or mechanical means, including information storage and retrieval systems, without written permission from the publisher, except in the case of a reviewer, who may quote brief passages embodied in critical articles or in a review.
First edition, 2025

Library and Archives Canada Cataloguing in Publication
First Picture Dictionary - Animals (Japanese English Bilingual edition)
ISBN: 978-1-83416-591-2 paperback
ISBN: 978-1-83416-592-9 hardcover
ISBN: 978-1-83416-590-5 eBook

やせいの どうぶつ
Wild Animals

らいおん
Lion

とら
Tiger

きりん
Giraffe

◆ きりんは りくじょうで いちばん せのたかい どうぶつ です。
✦ *A giraffe is the tallest animal on land.*

ぞう
Elephant

さる
Monkey

やせいの どうぶつ
Wild Animals

かば Hippopotamus

ぱんだ Panda

きつね Fox

さい Rhino

しか Deer

へらじか
Moose

おおかみ
Wolf

✦へらじかは およぐのが とくいで、
みずの なかにも もぐって
しょくぶつを たべます。
 ✦*A moose is a great swimmer and can dive underwater to eat plants!*

りす
Squirrel

こあら
Koala

✦りすは ふゆのために どんぐりを
かくしますが、どこにおいたか
わすれることが あります。
 ✦*A squirrel hides nuts for winter, but sometimes forgets where it put them!*

ごりら
Gorilla

ぺっと
Pets

かなりあ
Canary

✦かえるは はだでも はいでも いきを することが できます。
✦*A frog can breathe through its skin as well as its lungs!*

もるもっと
Guinea Pig

かえる
Frog

はむすたー
Hamster

きんぎょ
Goldfish

いぬ
Dog

✦おうむの なかには、ことばを
まねたり、にんげんみたいに
わらったり するものも います。
✦*Some parrots can copy words and even laugh like a human!*

おうむ
Parrot

ねこ
Cat

のうじょうの どうぶつ
Animals at the Farm

うし
Cow

にわとり
Chicken

あひる
Duck

ひつじ
Sheep

うま
Horse

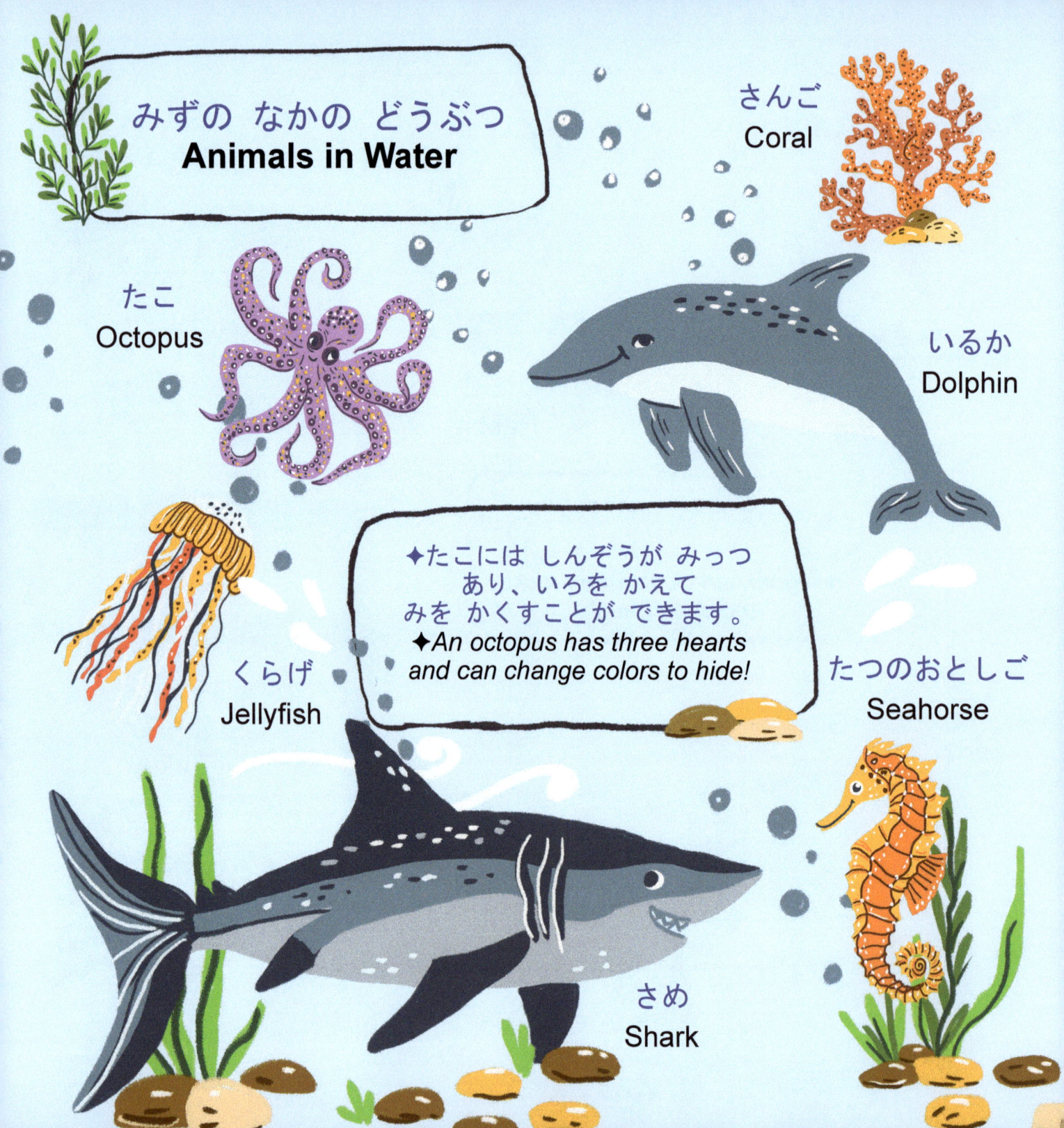

か
Mosquito

とんぼ
Dragonfly

✦とんぼは ちきゅうに さいしょに
あらわれた むしの ひとつで、
きょうりゅうよりも まえからいました。
✦A dragonfly was one of the first insects on Earth, even before dinosaurs!

はち
Bee

ちょうちょ
Butterfly

てんとうむし
Ladybug

あなぐま
Badger

やまあらし
Porcupine

まーもっと
Groundhog

✦とかげは しっぽが とれても あたらしく はえかわります。
✦*A lizard can grow a new tail if it loses one!*

とかげ
Lizard

あり
Ant

ちいさい どうぶつ
Small Animals

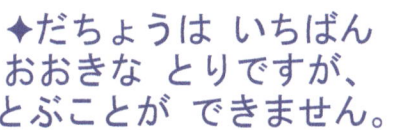

かめれおん
Chameleon

くも
Spider

✦だちょうは いちばん おおきな とりですが、 とぶことが できません。
✦*An ostrich is the biggest bird, but it cannot fly!*

はち
Bee

✦かたつむりは せなかに じぶんの いえを のせて、とても ゆっくり うごきます。
✦*A snail carries its home on its back and moves very slowly.*

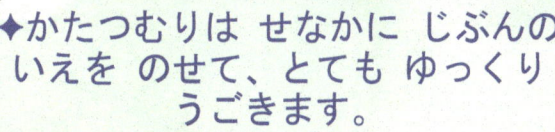

かたつむり
Snail

ねずみ
Mouse

しずかな どうぶつ
Quiet Animals

かめ
Turtle

てんとうむし
Ladybug

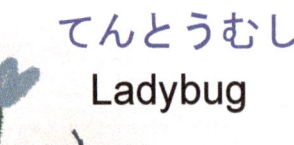

✦かめは りくでも みずの なか でも いきられます。
✦*A turtle can live both on land and in water.*

さかな
Fish

とかげ
Lizard

ふくろう
Owl

こうもり
Bat

✦ふくろうは よるに えものを
さがし、みみで おとを
ききわけます。
✦*An owl hunts at night and uses its hearing to find food!*

✦ほたるは よるに
ひかって ほかの
ほたるを さがします。
✦*A firefly glows at night to find other fireflies.*

あらいぐま
Raccoon

たらんちゅら
Tarantula

いろとりどりの どうぶつ
Colorful Animals

ふらみんごは
ぴんくいろ
です。
A flamingo is pink

ふくろうは
ちゃいろ です。
An owl is brown

はくちょうは
しろいろ です。
A swan is white

たこは　むらさきいろ　です。
An octopus is purple

かえるは
みどりいろ　です。
A frog is green

> ✦ かえるは みどりいろ なので、
> はっぱの あいだに かくれる
> ことが できます。
> ✦ *A frog is green, so it can hide among the leaves.*

どうぶつの おやこ
Animals and Their Babies

うし と こうし
Cow and Calf

ねこ と こねこ
Cat and Kitten

にわとり と ひよこ
Chicken and Chick

✦ ひよこは たまごから かえるまえに、おかあさんと おしゃべり します。
✦ *A chick talks to its mother even before it hatches.*

いぬ と こいぬ
Dog and Puppy

ちょうちょ と けむし
Butterfly and Caterpillar

ひつじ と こひつじ
Sheep and Lamb

うま と こうま
Horse and Foal

ぶた と こぶた
Pig and Piglet

やぎ と こやぎ
Goat and Kid

www.ingramcontent.com/pod-product-compliance
Lightning Source LLC
LaVergne TN
LVHW072101060526
838200LV00061B/4786